dealing with
difficult people
easily

Karen Mannering

For UK order enquiries: please contact Bookprint Ltd,
130 Milton Park, Abingdon, Oxon OX14 4SB.
Telephone: +44 (0) 1235 827720. *Fax*: +44 (0) 1235 400454.
Lines are open from 09.00–17.00, Monday to Saturday, with a
24-hour message answering service. Details about our titles
and how to order are available at www.hoddereducation.com

British Library Cataloguing in Publication Data: a catalogue record for this
title is available from the British Library.

First published in UK 2011 by Hodder Education, part of Hachette UK,
338 Euston Road, London NW1 3BH.

Typeset by MPS Limited, a Macmillan Company.

Printed in Great Britain for Hodder Education, an Hachette UK Company,
338 Euston Road, London NW1 3BH, by CPI Cox & Wyman, Reading,
Berkshire RG1 8EX.

The publisher has used its best endeavours to ensure that the URLs for external
websites referred to in this book are correct and active at the time of going to
press. However, the publisher and the author have no responsibility for the
websites and can make no guarantee that a site will remain live or that the
content will remain relevant, decent or appropriate.

Hachette UK's policy is to use papers that are natural, renewable and recyclable
products and made from wood grown in sustainable forests. The logging
and manufacturing processes are expected to conform to the environmental
regulations of the country of origin.

Impression number   10 9 8 7 6 5 4 3 2 1
Year   2015 2014 2013 2012 2011

Contents

1

what do we mean by a difficult person?

In this chapter we will be looking at what we mean by a 'difficult person' and face some home truths about what constitutes labelling others as 'difficult'. We will also look at a range of acknowledged types of behaviour that you may see every day around you, and offer up some quick tips as to how to deal initially with these people.

This is an incredible skill to add to your repertoire as increasingly more business is hampered by poor relationships than by faulty products. Initially you may have picked this book up because you know of someone you would like help with, but by putting time and effort into adding these techniques to your skill set, you will find that improvement seeps into all spheres of your business life. By exacting effort in one area, other areas will benefit too.

Who are the difficult people in your life? How do you decide that they are 'difficult'? Is it an instant feeling you get about someone or the result of a degenerating relationship? Is it about personalities or business?

You can choose your friends but not your work colleagues and when difficult people are in your team, you simply have to find a way forward.

The *Oxford English Dictionary* defines 'difficult' as being 'troublesome, perplexing, unaccommodating, stubborn', and indeed these are some of the types of people we will be discussing, together with those who are aggressive, selfish, negative, overly accommodating, insecure and high maintenance.

However, before we look at individual traits we need to establish some facts.

The 'One Universal Truth'

There is one universal truth that we need to accept before we can proceed:

There is no quick fix or magic wand that changes the behaviour of others.

You may have seen 'mind benders' and hypnotists on the stage and television, but as a qualified clinical hypno-psychotherapist I can tell you that there are no quick fixes to instant behavioural change, and any behavioural modification must be desired by the person concerned. In short, they will have found good reasons for displaying the type of behaviour they exhibit – it works for them and they get what they want. We need to show them that there is another way that not only also works, but is even more effective.

So if we cannot change everyone to our preferred way of behaving, where does that leave us? Well, the only thing that we can effectively change is ourselves – our own behaviour. This means having a number of techniques to hand and being open to try flexible approaches in applying them.

At this point you might be thinking that you picked up this book to change other people, not to have to change yourself. After all the problem is 'out there', isn't it? Not in here with you. Behaviour is a type of communicational dance, as we will see below, and the quality of the dance depends heavily on both partners.

Your role in the dynamic

Almost every time I am involved in mediation or some kind of dispute, I am called upon to change the behaviour of the other person because they are being difficult. It is so easy to think that every problem is because of the other person's 'difficult' personality, but in every interaction we cannot separate ourselves (or anyone else involved) from the dynamic.

What do I mean? Imagine you are walking down a corridor near to your office and you see two colleagues having a conversation about a third person. They are speaking and gesturing in ways they can both understand. As you pass you hear something of interest and decide to join the conversation. Suddenly the conversational rules need to change to accommodate you being present. Your colleagues may use different phrases or examples to illustrate their conversation, and if you are in any way related to or a friend of any of the characters being discussed, they will be very careful as to how they express their opinions. The point here is that you have had an impact on the way the communication can continue, that cannot be ignored. The conversational 'dance' has changed to accommodate a third 'dancer' and therefore the rules of the dance need to change.

The fact that we are part of the dynamic in any interaction means that we need to consider our own behaviour (verbal and non-verbal) at all times. We need to take full responsibility for the things we say and do to make sure we are part of the solution rather than a continuation of the problem.

Different types of difficult behaviour

To describe someone as 'difficult' is all encompassing. However, the degree or nature of the difficulty can vary from person to person. Let's look at a number of typically difficult behaviours here and see where these people may be coming from, as sometimes an insight into their behaviour can help us understand them, and therefore consequently deal with them, better.

Remember that popular psychology tells us that we must have some kind of reward for perpetuating our behaviour, and therefore an insight to where the motivation may come from is useful.

Aggressive people

You may be very well aware of aggressive people already – they stand tall, make a lot of noise and generally try to frighten and intimidate those about them. Of all the difficult types of people, aggressives make their presence widely known and are possibly the most openly feared of all the types.

But although they can make a big noise, which makes them scary, they are the WYSIWYGs of the business world. In other words, what you see is what you get. This obvious 'front' to their behaviour makes them easier to handle than some of their more devious counterparts. If you can get past the noise, then you might find out what is going on.

Aggressives need a firm stance. You have to stand up to them and be clear about how their behaviour affects you and others. Many aggressives appear to be astounded when told that their behaviour strikes fear into others; they feel they are being nothing more than vocally assertive. This mismatch in perceptions needs to be explored in detail before change can begin to take place.

Harassment laws are in place to prevent bullying in the workplace, and managers need to discuss this openly with all staff.

Know-it-alls

The main aspect of the know-it-all appears to be their irritating obsession with knowing everything, but slightly more worrying is their inability to listen. These are not the specialists known in every business, they are the busy bodies whom you find it difficult to stop once they are on a roll. Know-it-alls jump in before you have even finished your sentence, such is their keenness to demonstrate that they truly do know it all, and to state their claim to this knowledge before anyone else speaks. This means that they are not listening to the tail end of your message. That could be a problem, especially if you have designed a punchy ending or have left the most significant facts until last.

Below the surface of the know-it-all is the child who needs to feel important. They are searching for recognition that comes with information.

Know-it-alls need lots of reassurance; they need to feel important. Ways to deal with this could include:

* harnessing some of their enthusiasm by praising their knowledge
* balancing that out by praising others at the same time too
* being assertive in stopping them interrupting or cutting across you by asking them to allow you to finish each section of what you are trying to say
* giving feedback on their behaviour and how it affects you.

Selfish people

Selfish people don't share and that means anything from a pencil sharpener to a business idea. There may be a number of reasons for this – perhaps they had trouble sharing as children, perhaps they have never had to, and so now are unsure how. This may not be an issue for them in their private lives. However, when we are considering a work situation, items at work often have status values, and whether we share them or not gives an insight as to how comfortable we are about our own individuality. Staff can become very protective of the chair they sit in, which workstation they use, and whether they have to share an office or not.

Careful questioning may offer useful insight for the individual, and at the same time will give the message that this behaviour is not viewed favourably, at least within the business setting.

In the first instance:
* identify what exactly they are being selfish about (ideas, items, furniture)
* speak to them about how they see their identity in the team
* challenge them with their behaviour and try to find out what they think they will lose by sharing
* encourage them by bolstering their own ego and place in the team
* give them more joint projects where they have to work with someone else to achieve a successful outcome.

Negative people

Everyone knows someone who is negative but before you label them a complete 'nay sayer', consider that it may be a defence mechanism to prevent them from being rejected, shocked or hurt. Nevertheless, their behaviour can rankle and their effect can be widespread.

Negative people bring not only you but also the whole team down. Their glass is always half empty and they take pleasure in providing everyone with the 'worst case' scenarios at every opportunity. Rather than viewing their comments as negative, they often reason that they are merely being more realistic about events.

It would be almost impossible to change a fully negative person into a positive one so you are trying to make slight changes:
* Don't put them down. Instead acknowledge their views and then offer a counter approach, for example, 'Yes, this may fail, but I'm going to give it my best shot anyway.'
* Try to phrase suggestions in a positive format for them, such as, 'I'm sure you won't mind helping out on this task.'
* Acknowledge their role in the team: 'We need someone to be devil's advocate here, just to make sure we are on the right road. What about you, Mary? Challenge these ideas and let's see if they stand up to scrutiny.'
* If their negativity has a profound effect on the group, you may need to speak to them on a one-to-one basis but

make sure the conversation sticks to their comments and behaviours and is not personal.

Passive people and passive-aggressives

Passive people do not join in activities; they prefer to sit on the sidelines. They may not enter into team discussions, preferring to say nothing in the belief that if they say nothing they will not be wrong. They are often passive in all parts of their life, believing that great things happen only to other people, and that everyone else has far more power to make changes than they have.

Passivity is often linked to low self-esteem and therefore passive people need to:

* have their role acknowledged in the team
* be given specific pieces of work to undertake, bring back and discuss (to encourage them to engage)
* have positive feedback from everyone
* be encouraged to take an active part in meetings.

Their far more sinister partners are the passive-aggressives. They are the ones who say nothing in the meeting but mutter aggressive comments under their breath. In a sense they are cowards, hiding their comments behind their hand or papers. They can do a lot of damage in a team because they appear demure during the meeting but then out comes the poison later. If caught they often revert to childish behaviour, 'What me? I never said anything!'

When dealing with passive-aggressives you need to:

* have hard evidence of what they said and when they said it (this can be tricky because they cover their tracks well)
* confront them with their comments, and ask them for the reasons behind their behaviour
* explain the way in which their bad behaviour affects the team (including team morale)
* ask them in future to speak up with their comments within the meeting, so that you have a chance to discuss all matters at the time and they can be minuted if appropriate.

Passive-aggressives are not easy to stop, as their behaviour may have become ingrained. However, it is not to be tolerated. Refer them to any policies you may have on misconduct and start keeping notes.

Overly accommodating people

These people can be difficult in that they desperately want to please. They often have low self-esteem and can be annoyingly attentive in their need to be of use to someone else. It is not difficult to place these people under extreme pressure and overwork them because they say nothing until they become resentful or collapse. If you ask them to do a task they often rush off to do it immediately and leave their other work (which may not have been the best way to do it or the most efficient use of time). They are desperately seeking approval and may become depressed if they don't get the thanks they feel they deserve. In a sense they are like a dog wanting a stick to be thrown and expecting a pat in return for its retrieval.

Overly accommodating people need:
* to be valued – their self-esteem needs a big lift so work on building their inner confidence
* to know about boundaries – set times when they cannot gain access to you. Have a code such as putting up a sign for when you must not be interrupted
* to be given time management and assertiveness training – this will enable them to set their priorities for the day and help stick to them
* a significant project of their own to work on so that they achieve a solid outcome
* regular workplace monitoring to ensure they do not overwork.

Insecure people

Insecurity can manifest itself in a number of ways. On the one hand the insecure member of staff may be quiet and hang back from the rest of the team, or conversely they may compensate by being overly aggressive.

Insecure people need:
* appropriate questioning to find out where their insecurities lie
* lots of support, both physically and psychologically
* ongoing confidence building and esteem strengthening
* high quality feedback.

High maintenance people

High maintenance people are just that, they take up all your time. This may be because they are demanding attention or just very needy. High maintenance behaviour comes from a number or sources. They could have been an only child, used to a continuous audience, or perhaps they were born into a large family where only the one who shouts the loudest gets heard. If they are fairly young, they may even not know that this type of behaviour is not relevant in a work setting.

High maintenance people need:
* clear boundaries – they need to know when they can and cannot approach you. Consider setting some times of the day when you are not to be disturbed
* to know that they are doing their job properly – give them lots of good quality feedback and written notes in one-to-one sessions
* to be faced with their behaviour and told that it is untenable – but be given an opportunity to explain and start afresh
* to perhaps have a secret signal or sign that you can do to indicate that they have had enough of your time. It will allow them to withdraw with their self-esteem intact.

2

is there any way that I can read people?

Dealing with people we perceive to be difficult is a distinct skill and one that everyone can learn. Our behaviour is more predictable than we might initially think, and that means so is the behaviour of others, so, learn to sharpen your observational skills!

We may not be able to become mind readers but we can learn strategies that people commonly use, and then identify the 'triggers' that signal difficult behaviour, so that you have time to select the appropriate response. Whereas these may not be the same in everyone, there is a range of 'tells' and when we learn those, people are remarkably consistent in the ones they use. These 'tells' give us insight into the behaviour that might follow, and from that we can select a strategy. Already, by doing this, you are streets ahead of others who might just take the behaviour at face value each time.

Wouldn't it be great to be able to read what people are thinking? If it were possible, then perhaps we could head off any of the difficulties in their behaviour. Well, the good news is that the information is present if we know where to look for it, and if we take the effort to look for it. Yes, that's right, it takes real effort on our part because we are not necessarily used to using the intuitive side of our nature on a daily basis.

Visual 'tells'

Do faces and bodies give away signals? Can we tell whether someone is going to be an awkward customer just by looking at them? Certainly some people look more disagreeable than others, but is that always a reliable indication of their mood? I'm sure you will have experienced meeting someone who you initially thought to be cantankerous, only to find them charming when you got to know them. Always be cautious about jumping to conclusions with such unqualified 'information'.

Facially speaking

The study of body language comes from a mixture of:
* anthropology (the study of animal behaviour)
* neuro-linguistic programming (the study of the interconnectivity between the brain and our language), and
* social psychology (where the social setting and people involved may affect the behaviour).

It is no exact science but certain theories have been shown to be most reliable. Experiments into facial recognition have identified five major facial 'tells' that are common all over the world. They are:
* sadness
* fear
* happiness
* disgust
* anger.

The miraculous thing about this is that it is an innate quality that appears to cross cultures and boundaries, even in those cultures who have less expressive faces themselves. Therefore you most certainly *will* recognise these emotions when you see them, giving you pre-preparation time to greet the person in the most appropriate manner. For example, if you see someone coming towards you displaying an angry facial configuration, consider that they are just that – angry – and greet them with concern for their problem, rather than ignoring such basic facial tells and greeting them with a sunny smile.

The face is a very important part of the body as it is the showcase for many of our emotions.

There are a number of facial 'tells' that, although not proven conclusively, are common across a wide proportion of people. For example, when many people think or ponder on a response, their eyes go slightly up to their left. It can vary from a slight movement to a strong and lengthy one. This is thought to be the case because to consider all aspects of an issue or question, people need to access the left side of their brain, which takes on a more logical function, storing large amounts of data in streams and connections that need to be searched. (Although the brain is very interconnected, the right side is thought to deal mainly with more abstract, immediate and creative data.) Ask your colleagues a question that requires them to think hard to answer (perhaps about something that may have happened in their childhood) and see whether this is true of them. It may only be a tiny movement, but look for that quick flick of the pupil before the eyes return to focus on you. If you find that this is correct for your particular work colleagues you will always be able to see whether they are really considering your new proposal fully – or just saying they are. Neuro-linguistic programming (NLP) is the study of brain-to-verbal communication. It also incorporates body language nuances, and that includes eye movement. NLP studies teach us that different parts of the brain are responsible for handling different aspects of thought processes, and that the eyes move to indicate whatever thought process is being used.

Many people are aware that when we are genuinely interested in someone, our pupils dilate. This research has been undertaken extensively, especially in dating situations, and found to be amazingly accurate. However, the situation does not have to be about physical attraction. Gazing at a desirable watch, piece of jewellery, or just finding someone interesting would have the same effect. Again you can use this information to your advantage with difficult people. Look into their eyes. Are they really interested in you, your ideas and presentations or just paying lip service to them?

Body giveaways

The face is not the only information hot spot. Bodies generate volumes of information. The way we stand, move, twist and turn and, of course, our arm gestures, tell anyone willing to notice just what we really think. For example, when we like someone we move in rapport with them. Moving in rapport simply means that we use similar gestures and positioning of the body, which communicates as 'you are just like me'.

Much has been written concerning body language and the meanings attributed to certain gestures, some of it helpful and some of it less so. It is very difficult to generalise in many cases as, being very sophisticated and complex animals, we even create our own 'designer' body tells that work only for us.

Another area where our body language can give us away is in the upper torso. A large number of people carry tension in their neck muscles. This means that when someone feels tense or under pressure, their shoulders are raised a little higher than normal, and the whole upper torso becomes stiff and less flexible. This can result in the person having a more solid but 'wooden' look that is perceptible to others. Similarly, if someone is coming towards you in an aggressive manner, they often pull themselves up to their full height and make their upper body as wide as possible. It is the human equivalent of having your feathers or fur stand on end. One thing that is helpful to know when dealing with someone demonstrating this body position (through whatever circumstance) is that maintaining it is incredibly energy consuming. In fact no one can maintain this state indefinitely, and when they do 'come down' they will be physically depleted. Their energy is sapped, they are tired, and in extreme circumstances they may even cry. Although they cannot stay in this high state of anger indefinitely, they need to deal with handling the resulting loss of energy in a dignified way. Interrupting, trying to speak over them, or appearing falsely sympathetic will either increase their anger further to explosion point or induce them to walk out, neither of which will solve the situation.

Hands and arms are another body tell. Look at the person you are speaking to. Are their hands giving wide expansive gestures or are they tightly in a ball? Are they relaxed to the sides or gesturing wildly and indicating some form of excitement? Look where they are in relation to the rest of the body and at the tension in the fingers. The person in front of you may not be shouting but if their hands are tightly clenched and their knuckles are white, they may be near to boiling point.

Lies, damned lies and statistics

The thing that we all want to know is whether there are any certain 'tells' that expose liars. Scratching that itch around the nose area and in fact any movement of the hands around the nose and mouth area tend to be interpreted as lying 'tells' but be careful – the other person may just have an itchy nose!

If there are any sure signs, all I can say is that the police and the courts would find them most interesting! Hands around and covering the mouth, rubbing of the back of the neck, or a failure to make eye contact may represent shifty or evasive behaviour but it would be a significant leap to accuse that person of lying. Even lie detectors that measure the amount of sweat produced when you are asked questions while testing your blood pressure can be fooled by some accomplished liars. The message here, then, is to use your body language interpreting skills to decipher what you can, but also not to make huge assumptions. You could be terribly wrong and make the situation far worse than it already is.

Verbal 'tells'

Verbal communication is often referred to as a dance. It has a broad set of rules; I will speak for a minute or so while you listen, then I shall be quiet while you give your response for a minute or so, and so we go on taking it in turns, batting our comments back and forth like a polite tennis match. While the dance is adhered to, there is no problem, each of us knows our role and our place. However, if the dance is disrupted by either partner not dancing 'by the rules', perhaps by shouting, sulking, or not understanding the dance correctly (such as talking across each other or shouting to get attention rather than in anger), then confusion will break out.

Difficult verbal situations include those with people who shout and also those who are unnervingly quiet. Shouters tend to fall into two main types: those whose voices rise because they are excited or shout the odd command to make a point, and those who use continued shouting as an instrument of aggression. Admittedly they may appear very scary at first, but it is often a very short interaction, and when you understand their tactics and the fact that it is actually they who are having trouble coping, you may feel secure in having the moral high ground.

Silent people are very different. It does not take much energy to be silent and so they can maintain their silence for a very long time. This, combined with the fact that they clearly have the most control over the situation, makes them much more difficult to deal with. Communication is essential to sort out life's problems and a refusal to speak shows obstinacy and a total lack of willingness to move towards a solution. Where you are faced with a wall of silence in a work situation, you will need to deal with it as a behavioural issue through your organization's policies. Communication is essential in business and a refusal to communicate effectively may be a disciplinary issue.

Look and learn

We have established that some people are more prone to visual and verbal 'tells' than others, and that these 'tells' may be exhibited in different ways. However, one thing we do know is that, unless people are made aware of these 'tells' or habits, they will continue to do them. They are amazingly consistent in the individual, with each individual displaying their own version of one or more anxiety tells. The lesson therefore is twofold. Firstly, pay close attention to the tells of others and make a mental note of them. You will then be in an excellent position to 'read' the emotions of your colleagues during a difficult interaction. Secondly, be very aware of your own signals. You may have others watching you and you may be giving too much away that is to their advantage.

Conclusion

We all move and interact with each other on a number of levels including subliminally. The main problem is that when we meet someone who is either being difficult or we know to be difficult, we forget to look for the signals that give us enhanced information regarding their temperament at that time. There are a number of very common 'tells' that reveal certain anxieties, and we can then change our approach in line with what is being exhibited. However, that anxiety may be there for a considerable number of different reasons, and we need good verbal communication if we want to reconcile any differences.

3

difficult employees – how do I deal with them?

Being a manager of people is never easy. 'If only people were like machines,' I hear managers say, 'I would be able to turn them off or take the batteries out!' If only life were that simple. The truth is that very little is achieved without people, and that means not only working alongside people but also having others work directly for you.

So much emotional investment is bound up in the psychological contract that staff have with their employers that there are bound to be sparks from time to time. Work is very complex today and productivity can be severely damaged through bad relationships with staff. While creating a comfortable environment is no guarantee of business success, creating an uncomfortable one certainly will fail, and possibly leave you open to a legal challenge. Demonstrate to your employees your respect by considering how to get the most from your employees.

Sometimes when we become managers we are in the fortunate position of being able to select our team members, but more likely we may inherit a team. This could happen for a number of reasons: perhaps we are moving into a job where we are replacing the manager and the team is already in place, or it could be that we have been brought in as a new manager especially to take over a tricky team.

There is a third scenario, that the team is indeed new but the people in it are disaffected characters from other parts of the organisation. Treat your new team or employees as a new blank canvas, and draw your own conclusions from their current behaviour, not the past.

Building the relationship right from the start

Not everyone comes to work to have a jolly time. Neither does everyone come to work brimming with enthusiasm every day. Although motivation to work is not entirely about money, there is no doubt that we need money in our lives to pay the bills. There is also the need for people to work towards something – a goal – and feel that their work is noble in its move towards completing a project. We will look at motivation later but the money angle does not go away and it pays to be realistic about people if you are going to build a meaningful relationship with your employees.

Like all relationships, things can get off to a good or bad start, and this can set the tone for the rest of the relationship. This should not mean that you have to walk around as if on egg shells, but early actions leave lasting impressions that may be more difficult to erase later on. Far better to create a strong, positive force initially, than to have to try to salvage the situation later on.

Setting the 'personality' of your team

Leadership is essential and will help give your team or staff group a personality. What do I mean by personality? You must have noticed how some teams work better than others; how some staff members prefer to work for certain managers. Somehow working in one team can feel very different from working with another.

Figure 1 *The team personality.*

There are three things you need to consider here:
* You – will have your own leadership style that you need to bring to the team (or your employees).
* The organisation – has its own personality (including its values) that you need to operate within.
* The team – when you introduce anyone new into an existing staff group, the dynamic will change.

Why is this important? Because all three factors combine to make up the team personality (see Figure 1) and the teams that have a feel good factor are the ones that never have a problem finding staff, in fact staff often clamber to join them. They run efficiently and effectively, and usually have low turnover of staff, thus saving your time later on recruitment. When staff start coming to you to ask when there might be vacancies in your team, you know you are working in the right direction.

Ensuring the right fit of role to succeed

As mentioned earlier, attracting the right staff to work with you is crucial, but not always possible. However, what you will find is that, as your ability to work well with people fuels your reputation, there will be people seeking you out and literally knocking on your door. After a while, as your reputation grows, everyone will want to work for the manager who took on a difficult team and won them over.

If you are inheriting a team or group of employees you may think that you can do little except carry on where the previous manager left off. Absolutely not – if you always do what you always did, you will always get what you always got. Time for a total rethink and it is back to roles once again. How would you like your team or staff to be organised? What would work best for the business? Do certain roles need more interaction than others?

Matching motivation

The right cognitive approach is also essential. We all come to work for different reasons and others may not be as motivated as ourselves, or at least motivated by the same things. You may be excited by being a new manager and keen to try out some of your theories, but your employees may be feeling apprehensive. After all, you are an unknown quantity for them, and there is a common perception that all change is negative. You will be seen as the change maker, and this could cause a temporary barrier between you and your staff.

You need to find out more about your employees. Why do they come to work? Apart from the obvious financial benefit, what do they personally gain from being there? Who do they interact with/lunch with? What aspects of the job do they like/dislike? Where do they hope to go in their career? How do they think you can help them get there?

This 'getting to know you' approach will not just help to give you broad information about your employees but will specifically target their motivation drivers. When you know what brings people into work, you can build some of that into their day-to-day working environment.

Personality profiling

The idea that people can operate in a set number of ways that enable others to predict their behaviour is not new. Thousands of years ago the Greeks used a system of four humours to describe personality types:

* Sanguine – the Artisan, courageous, hopeful and amorous
* Melancholic – the Rationalist, despondent, sleepless and irritable
* Phlegmatic – the Idealist, calm and unemotional
* Choleric – the Guardian, easily angered and bad tempered.

Modern psychologists have devised further categorisation. Work since the 1940s has produced five scales that nearly all personality questionnaires now include as the basis of their interpretation. These five scales are known as the Big Five, and measure:

* Extroversion
* Neuroticism/Anxiety
* Openness to experience/Conformity
* Agreeableness/Tender vs Tough-mindedness
* Conscientiousness.

Whereas we do not want to 'pigeon-hole' people, some information concerning your employees' personality type could be very useful for helping you to know the best way to manage them.

So is it a good idea to put everyone through a personality questionnaire? They have a dual purpose: you learn more about your staff but, perhaps even more importantly, they learn more about themselves. Self-knowledge leaves an open door for dealing with difficult behaviour. When anyone is curious to discover more about themselves, it is a good time to discuss how their behaviour also affects the people around them. Sometimes a conversation opener is what we need to approach an uncomfortable issue.

If personality profiles could help you and your employees, then better be safe than sorry, and being safe means using:

* a well-documented testing procedure – never buy a product off the shelf. It will not have been subjected to the rigorous testing of the major tests
* a practitioner who can advise and run the tests for you – all tests do not measure the same aspects of personality and therefore you need to know that you are measuring the traits that you have identified as being useful in the job role.

A practitioner needs to hold a Level B certificate in psychometrics to ensure they are aware not only of how the test operates but also are able to give high quality interpretation of the results and provide feedback. A list of registered practitioners can be obtained from the British Psychological Society (BPS).

Never try to cut corners by using tests without expert help. Should you subsequently find yourself accused of constructive dismissal, or in an Employment Tribunal, the fact that you were dabbling in areas you are not qualified in will stand against you.

Identifying personal influencers

In every group there are influencers and disrupters, and in some sense the qualities they bring to each of these roles are similar. In essence these people have some form of people power in that they are able to influence others, sometimes positively and sometimes negatively. After all, if they had no influence and were ignored, they would not be able to stir things up for either good or bad.

French and Ravens (1960) identified the following power bases:

* Reward power: the ability to give or take away praise, resources, funding, promotion.
* Coercive power: the ability to punish and reprimand.
* Legitimate power: from one's position or office.
* Expert power: the use of superior knowledge and skills.
* Referent power: where others seek the leader's approval.
* Information power: to give, withhold or filter information.
* Connection power: perceived to be in close contact with influential people.
* Ascribed power: accurate or distorted attributions of power ascribed to another person.

The reason for identifying the power play in employee groups is to tap into their skills and work with them rather than against them.

When you allow influencers to do their work, it is crucial that you do not intervene or make your own announcement. You need to back off and allow them time and space to weave their magic web. For the manager, this letting go might not seem natural. You may feel that you would rather wade in and exert your own personality as manager. After all, you have the most current appreciation of the situation. But resist. Allow your influencer to do the hard work for you and you may find that when it comes to the meeting, the people in front of you are already half way to being persuaded of the idea, and just need your final comments to add authority.

Everyone is entitled to their views regarding any work decision, but they are not entitled to disrupt the entire team because of those views. Although there are many unwritten rules governing our behaviour, a level of social behaviour is expected in the workplace. You may even have a charter naming some such behaviours, represented as 'respect for others' or similar codes of conduct. In many organisations, acting in an antisocial manner or displaying poor or disruptive behaviour is considered misconduct.

Conclusion

You may have a team of diverse employees but you need to use your skill to identify difficult behaviour and deal with it. Really get to know your employees as individuals, find out their career histories, their motivations, and their personalities. Always look for a reason behind poor behaviour and consider whether it is justified or not. If it is not and it is the first occasion, have a quiet word. If it has happened a couple of times, set targets, but if it is an ongoing problem it must be picked up through the correct organisational procedure. If you have to go down this route, make sure you keep a written record of all the incident times, and the measures you took at each point on the way. This would be your evidence if necessary.

4

difficult managers – how do I deal with them?

Having a difficult manager can add a level of complexity that just creates additional tension. We expect managers to support staff rather than add more pressure, but the reality is that some managers just add to the difficulty of work rather than take away from it. There is also the additional difficulty of them being the gateway to future pay rises, promotion opportunities and ultimately providing a reference for you if you decide to move on.

However, we need to look not only at the actual behaviour but seek to understand some of the issues in being a manager. Through understanding, we may be able to accept the behaviour (even though we may not agree with it) – then we can make decisions about our future relationship with that particular manager. This is not an excuse for poor behaviour but gives you choices at a time when you feel disempowered.

Some of the biggest problems may not lie with the people you are managing but in your managers and senior managers.

There is no doubt that managers are in a superior position, and therefore in a position of power – with the power to ultimately hire and fire employees. It may also be that they own the organisation or have been senior there for a very long time. If your manager owns the organisation or company, and is behaving very badly to you, you need to think very clearly whether you really want to work for someone like that. Not only will they continue to treat you poorly but there is also the danger that you may slip into the practice of thinking this is natural, and therefore develop a similar style, to fit the culture.

The manager/worker relationship

Essentially the employer/employee relationship is one of a work-for-wage bargain. You will provide the work and for that you will receive a wage – all other facets of the job are open for negotiation. Employment law is also clear that you are entitled to guidance and training in aspects of your job and you, as a manager, have a duty of care for the staff who report to you. Your manager, however senior, also has this responsibility.

Within the context of difficult managers, identifying and strengthening our own personal power can help us gain the strength to deal with difficult situations. Personal power comes from within, can be made stronger and developed. Yes it can be dented, but it does not disappear and every knock back can result in it being stronger than before.

To strengthen your personal power core:
  * Let go of blame and guilt both for yourself and towards others.
  * Be forgiving.
  * Learn how to back off from a disagreement without becoming aggressive, even if the other person is.

* Don't apologise for anything that is not your fault.
* Shake off any feelings you have about winning or losing with your manager.
* Be firm in your values, beliefs and feelings.
* Learn and move on.

Consider the relationship between yourself and other managers (not just your own) very carefully.
* How do you interact with each other?
* What happens when you meet? (Not just at a superficial level – what body language is displayed?)
* When you speak do you look each other in the eye?
* How are requests/orders given? In what manner?
* What happens when things go wrong?
* How are problems reported to you and what are the likely penalties?

The answer to these questions will tell you about your relationship with senior staff and how they relate to you and your position.

What can you do to help build bridges in the relationship? Here are some first steps:
* Act quietly confident. If you really don't know something then, of course, ask.
* However, when you want to ask, then ask with confidence.
* Try to be personable. Reflect on any feedback you may have had in the past – whether you agreed with the giver or not, they may have had a point.
* Phrase your question as a request for shared activity. Instead of asking your own manager, 'How can I motivate my staff?' try suggesting, 'I would like to discuss with you some more ideas for motivating staff. I have my own ideas, but together I thought we may come up with some additional methods I could introduce.'

The view from the top

Every level of management has a different view. As managers move up in the organisation their 'view' becomes different. They may lose some of the individualism and concentrate more on the larger picture, for example, how the organisation is placed in the open market. It is important to be aware of this change of view because it affects not only you for the future, but also your dealings with senior managers, and it may explain why some of your communications have not been successful. Perhaps you are just not appreciating each other's 'view' and something that seems important to you may not even appear on a more senior manager's radar.

Remember: If you want to appeal to your manager for something, it is far better to couch the request in terms of their view of the world. For example, asking for new chairs for my team may not interest my manager and I may be brushed off, but couch it in terms of supporting the health and safety check that is happening next month, and my manager will be far more willing to listen because that falls more into their strategic role.

The other point here is that as soon as you become a manager or supervisor you become the filling in a sandwich. In other words, until that moment you only had to concern yourself with what your manager said and how your manager or supervisor felt about you and your work. As soon as you move up one rung and become that manager or supervisor, that is when you become the filling. You are suddenly managing both up and down. This is particularly evident when it comes to information. You have to become a filter. Your manager above you does not want or need to know every nuance about the staff in your care, and likewise you will not be passing on every word your manager says, down to the team.

Remember: Be guarded in the information you pass on and be aware that the view is very different from different levels in the organisation. When your manager looks at you blankly it could be because they do not understand why you have come to them with this information. It just might not be relevant to them.

At different levels, in addition to the differing priorities mentioned above, there are also differing pressure points and deadlines. You may be working to a weekly output plan but your direct manager may be working on an annual rolling programme, which requires different measuring and forecasting procedures. You may be happy if you go home at the end of the week with your team having met their targets for that period; your manager may be living under continual stress to deliver and perform on a schedule that appears to have no end.

To improve communication further you need to learn to speak in their own language as much as possible. If you need to raise a tactical issue, tie it in to one of your manager's outcomes. For example, if you wanted to speak to your manager about two workers constantly disagreeing, your manager may immediately think that you really should not be bothering them with such inconsequential piffle and should sort it out yourself. However, when you raise it as a concern that the end of quarter targets may not be met, then you will definitely have them listening! If you need your manager to listen to you, think through how you will phrase the message so that you capture their attention in the most effective method possible.

The other point here is to consider in detail how you present your information, such as phrasing information in as positive manner as possible. For example, rather than saying, 'It looks like Jim might be late with the report figures for tomorrow because they are so much more difficult than usual' and getting both you and Jim bawled out you could try, 'The new frameworks for the figures will lead us to a much more accurate assessment of where we are making positive changes, however, they seem to be taking a little longer than before and therefore, there may be a slight delay in getting them to you this week. If this continues to be a problem, can I suggest that we design a longer lead-in time to enable Jim to do a good job? I'm sure you will think the result is worth the extra time.' You may still get bawled out but it is unlikely Jim will be, and he will be forever grateful to you. There is always the possibility that you can 'sell' a mistake as an opportunity, and your staff will respect you for protecting them.

Internal politics

Internal politics are a fact of life. In many large companies managers need to position and reposition themselves constantly, and work can be an ever-changing landscape. It does not help that decisions do not always appear to be rational. You may feel that you are doing a good job and communicating well, only to be replaced by someone else. It therefore always pays to keep one eye on the horizon and build in some of your own support mechanisms. Three ideas to help are:

* Build a support group – this could be a networking group at a professional or personal level.
* Find a mentor – a mentor will help you not only by supporting you but also offering advice, help and information.
* Work to improve your skills level – this will give you knowledge and instant confidence.

When vast changes take place in organisations, most of the staff will start aligning themselves with whoever is the new power base. You need to think very carefully before you fully align your allegiance in any one direction (some organisations are more political than a Tudor court). Complicating the matter is that you may have very strong views that lead you in one direction and these may be unpopular. People can be much admired for their strength of view or vision but you need to be aware that you will be judged by that. If your view conflicts very strongly with your manager's, it can be a long and lonely fight. If that happens, you might be better to take your ideas somewhere else – only you will know.

Conflict with your boss is not very comfortable and you may need to ask yourself whether you need this level of hassle. Some of this will depend on how important the job is to you.

The key here is to work with your own levels. There are many different organisations and styles of working, and therefore if one organisation is not right for you, there are others that might be a better fit.

	High importance	Low importance
High levels of managerial conflict	You could feel like you are on an emotional rollercoaster. You may have to hang in there for your job and find coping mechanisms.	Look around for another job. You are being subjected to large amounts of negative conflict for no apparent gain.
Low levels of managerial conflict	You may be able to work in harmony here but make sure you instigate some creative thinking to introduce some spark.	You may want to stay if you value harmony but this role will not take your career further.

Figure 2 *Level of importance.*

Coping or escaping – what's it to be?

There are going to be times when you feel that the relationship you have with your own manager is not going to be workable due to their behaviour. Whatever type of difficult behaviour is being displayed, as long as it is not violent, you need to decide how to deal with it (see Figure 2).

In Figure 2, the first question deals with whether or not you can have an open and honest conversation with your manager. The second consideration, then, is whether the situation is likely to change. Even difficult work situations do eventually level out, and if this is the case, it might be worth seeing the situation for what it is – a temporary problem that will eventually fizzle out – and your manager may even feel grateful to you for hanging in there. The alternative is to leave, and it may be that this is the best course of action. However, this may not be so simple if you are 'trapped' in your job due to it being:

* a family run business
* an organisation with a brilliant reputation for your career (but a lousy culture)
* the only company in your area that specialises in this business area.

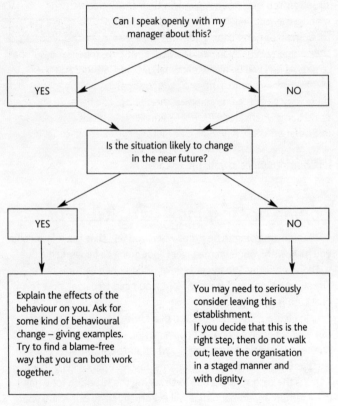

Figure 3 *Coping or escaping – what is it to be?*

Note: If the behaviour is violent in any way, please make sure that you take expert advice or report any incidents.

If any of these are the case then you cannot just leave and in reality we are looking at coping mechanisms until something changes or your manager leaves.

Conclusion

Having a difficult manager or boss puts you in a very tricky situation. You may not have known their true personality or management style when you joined the company. You have only three main options: coping, leaving, or changing your style to suit the company. What you decide will depend very much on a number of factors and will be a very personal decision. Although in your heart you may want to move on, life is not always so clear cut and there may be limited options. For this reason, and because you may move somewhere else with a boss equally as difficult (but perhaps in a different way), it pays to consider trying out some coping skills. They will stand you in good stead for dealing with so many different situations in your future career.

5

difficult colleagues – how do I deal with them?

Colleagues become more than just the people we work with. There is an expectation that we will all gel with colleagues and get along famously, whereas the truth may be somewhat different. Colleagues can demonstrate upfront confrontational behaviour or even be surreptitious and underhand in devaluing your role. You would not think that you were all working towards the good of the company – more that everyone is, to use a metaphor, paddling their own canoe. This behaviour may go on with or without the knowledge of your boss/manager, but leaves you feeling that perhaps this 'dream job' is more of a nightmare!

It is crucial for you to realise that you do not have to be a victim to this situation. There are actions you can do that may relieve matters or help considerably. Only when you have given matters every chance should you decide where your future lies.

The colleague relationship can be fraught with difficulty in itself. For a start your work colleagues, unlike friends in real life, are not necessarily people you choose to be with. You have to be productive together to get the work done, even if, on occasions, you feel that your skills and knowledge are superior to theirs. If that isn't enough you also have to keep one eye out for 'game play' where they may be after your job or, what you had considered to be, your natural progression.

The colleagues we are discussing here could be anyone from the people you meet at work to those you bring into the organisation to work alongside you. Perhaps you share an office or work near each other, or maybe you could have been put together to work on a project. Whatever the situation, or however you met, you all have a vested interest in the relationship. Work colleagues can be a great source of support and help but equally they can also cause a lot of anxiety.

Creating the right atmosphere at work

One of the biggest mistakes that people make with colleagues is to underestimate how their relationship affects the atmosphere at work.

It might be worth spending just a few moments thinking about what constitutes a bad atmosphere for you. Is it about people not speaking or speaking too much? Is it about having the wrong people around you every day? Or perhaps it is about a lack of respect or suspicion?

Ask yourself another set of questions, such as how would you like your working environment to be? Some people like air conditioning, others don't. For some people music in the background is soothing, for others it is an irritant. It all adds to the atmosphere at work.

If you like great ideas and a 'buzzing' feel to your day you need to surround yourself (or at least be able to get your 'fix' at some point during the day) with creative and 'happening' people. Negative colleagues will drain you, over-excitable colleagues will tire you in the long term, and overly playful colleagues may be better restricted to small doses. Think about your colleagues not only in the sense of 'do I like them?' but also in the sense of 'do they provide the atmosphere, ambience and stimulation I need to excel in my job?'.

Exploring your relationship

Now let's consider the curse of the Return of the Colleague. Okay, so you joined at the same time on the graduate scheme, or perhaps you worked together on that tricky project a couple of years ago. Now you are going to be working together again and it will be just the same, won't it? Or perhaps it will be even better.

People change. Time, life and experience change us all and most people will have had different experiences even in just one year that may radically impact on the way in which they work. Coupled with the fact that there may now be even more competition between you, or a power imbalance in some way, and we are set for fireworks.

Don't expect relationships to stay the same. The likelihood is that you will have moved on and so will they: you are back to the beginning, starting over and need to forge a new relationship. The good thing is that, if you are both able to be honest, knowing each other from the past can make a good base for the future.

Identifying what's in it for them

Behaviour is governed by our wants and needs. Freud postulated the concept of the 'pleasure principle', and our base need to satisfy this need. Freud would say that this need is a driver that governs all our decisions. What gives us pleasure is what we do. Even altruism, the act of selflessly putting others first, Freud would argue is governed by the pleasure principle. He would say that by putting others first, you were gaining satisfaction, the satisfaction of knowing that you have helped. So it is difficult to get away from this concept.

Now let's link this reward to emotions by trying a little exercise. Close your eyes and imagine feeling really good. It does not matter where or when, just the intensity of the feelings. Try to feel that intensity of pleasure throughout your entire body, from the top of your head to the tips of your toes. Now try to imagine that feeling ten times more intense, ten times more colourful, and ten times more pleasurable. Finally, link that feeling to a situation you don't much like, perhaps eating a certain vegetable or your rush hour trip in to work. See yourself in glorious technicolour enjoying the very thing that you don't normally enjoy, feeling deep pleasure and excitement for the task in hand. Now open your eyes. If you continued to do that exercise regularly, several times a day, you would find those excited feelings entering your mind and body when you come into contact with your given situation. Perhaps you will even start eating vegetables with great excitement! So, emotions can also be linked to behaviour.

However, not all associations are good. The other side of this coin is that behavioural psychologists believe that humans will go to enormous lengths to avoid what gives them pain or displeasure. If you see someone coming who you would rather not deal with, you will go to any length to avoid them. This is called our natural defence mechanism. We seek to avoid pain or discomfort in most circumstances, and it is the rational or irrational fear of that being present that causes us to avoid some serious communications.

Trying to identify each person's WIIFM drive can be very helpful, and you can do this subtly by asking them over a break time coffee, 'The project you are working on seems to be going very well, what personal satisfaction do you get from it?' or 'That looks good, how is this work going to help you in your career?' Sit back and see what unfolds. Their responses may surprise you.

Communicating pressure points at your level

There may be many times when you need to communicate pressure points and concerns at your level to other colleagues. It is not always acceptable to say that you feel stressed as that can be perceived as a weakness in some organisations. Therefore, before you cry on a colleague's shoulder in the rest room, think through a few options.

Let's get one aspect out of the way: it is all right to express your emotions. In fact, the people who are able to use their emotions to great effect have higher levels of emotional intelligence. Emotional intelligence is a concept made popular by Daniel Goleman in his book of the same title. In this he identified five main areas of emotional intelligence:

* Self awareness – knowing your own internal preferences and feelings.
* Self-regulation – managing those internal preferences and feelings.
* Motivation – emotional tendencies that guide or facilitate goals.
* Empathy – awareness of the feeling of others
* Social skills – the ability to induce a desirable response in others.

For example, one of the key factors required in business today is resilience. This is the need to be able to recover quickly from setbacks. Being able to reframe situations and think clearly in a difficult situation is another aspect of emotional intelligence. Resilience links directly with emotional intelligence as it taps into several of Goleman's key areas above.

However, demonstrating your emotional intelligence to others does not mean sobbing openly at the first sign of trouble. Emotions need to be kept in some form of balance to be considered genuine.

When going to colleagues is not always possible because of their other vested interests, then you need another outlet for gaining a sympathetic ear. A place where you can discuss your problems, and gain help with challenging questions. A safe wall to bounce ideas off can be crucial as there will be many occasions when you are simply too close to the problem to see the answer. In these instances, rather than go to a colleague, ask your manager about arranging for a mentor.

Mentors are often sounding boards, and can be either people from inside or outside the organisation. They tend to work specifically with work problems and processes (such as how to manage change at work) and bring a great deal of their own experience into the discussion. For this reason, mentors are often selected for their seniority of position, their high level of knowledge and their personal experience. Having a mentor can be hugely productive, for example, who else could you talk to confidentially if you were thinking of making changes at work, or with your team? Mentors can also provide advice on personal development, a factor that often gets forgotten in the turbulent world of work.

Finding commonalities and links

When dealing with other people at our own level, we need to communicate effectively and also build a sufficiently robust relationship that enables us to work together on joint projects. We do not need to be friends but it helps if, as mentioned above, we are not adversaries either. The shortest route to building quick relationships is through the identification of commonalities and links.

It makes us feel less isolated, more in touch with others, and is a boon for those who like to network. If you are ever at a networking event or need to make a connection with someone fast – perhaps you will soon be working together – the fastest way to success is to find that link, and use it to build a bridge of understanding between you both.

Being forgiving

Work colleagues will fall out. You may be competing for the same goal or cross each other over your work. Stress and pressure impact on how we interact with each other and the stage is set for miscommunication to occur. Metaphorical daggers are drawn and a stand-off seems inevitable. How can you ever work with this person again? How can you ever forgive their actions or words? When all is said and done, one of the biggest human skills is that of forgiveness. It is another feature that sets us apart from animals, and makes us far more sophisticated. Forgiveness is also a very personal judgement on a situation, and although those who forgive openly often appear to have the moral high ground, it has to come from the heart for it to be genuine.

We all judge other people all the time, and the only template we have available that we truly know well is ourselves. For this reason we often compare others to ourselves and their acts to those we would undertake. How many times have you heard people say with indignation, 'I wouldn't do that', even though what the person concerned is doing is not really wrong? Perhaps they have a different way of doing things or way of acting, but by retorting, 'I wouldn't do that', they are not just responding to the act itself, they are putting a value judgement on it, and this value judgement is usually 'I'm right and you are wrong'. The psychologist Berne expressed it slightly differently in his work on Transactional Analysis. He talked about four states:

1 I'm OK, you're not OK (as mentioned above)
2 I'm not OK, but you're OK
3 I'm not OK, you're not OK
4 I'm OK, you're OK

Let's look at these in more detail:

I'm OK, you're not OK – This is not a healthy state because it is passing judgement on the other person and finding them lacking. It shows an implied superiority, putting yourself above the other individual, and is no basis for mutual discussions at the same level.

I'm not OK, but you're OK – This demonstrates an empowering of the other person, detrimental to yourself. It demonstrates a lack of inner certainty and passivity – confident and assertive people do not provide other people with the ammunition to shoot them down!

I'm not OK, you're not OK – A very sad position where the individual cannot see good in themselves or others. They may be depressed or perhaps disenchanted, but whatever is the cause of this, it is not a healthy place to be.

I'm OK, you're OK – This is the healthiest state of all. It demonstrates balance and an acknowledgement of equality, in addition to mutual respect. We are both OK, we might have different ideas and opinions but they are both valid. It is in this state that we are able to forgive.

Letting go can be cathartic and cleansing; some people can dislike another colleague for years and they can't even remember how it all started. Ultimately they are only damaging themselves and bizarrely, there are occasions when the other person does not even know about it.

It is not always possible to forgive but where you can, you should, if only for your own health and wellbeing. We all walk the earth together and need to rely on each other from time to time. When something negative happens with a colleague, consider:

* You may be angry but is your level of wrath justified by the incident?
* How would it sound if you described the incident to someone else? Would it sound foolish?
* If someone were describing the situation to you, what would you recommend?
* How would you feel if that person was involved in a tragic accident on the way home from work that night?
* How would you feel if that person were suddenly promoted into the position of your boss?
* Do you honestly feel that continuing this feud is productive?
* Be honest, do you secretly gain pleasure from this?

It may be that you are holding on to this hurt because you gain from it in some way. Maintaining bad feelings about colleagues is common, albeit rarely productive. Be the first to show that you can forgive incidents and your relationships will flourish in the future.

Conclusion

The colleague relationship is full of flex and change. You could join the organisation and be put in a group of colleagues, perhaps on a graduate scheme, at the same level, and three years later some will have progressed and others will not. Professional colleagues are not always colleagues in the truest sense. Any friendship will be sorely tested through time and actions. Although no one should ever refrain from workplace friendships, it is foolish to ignore the dynamics that go on at collegial level, and how the seductive search for power often comes at the cost of someone else's fall.

Understanding the problems that can surround workplace colleague relationships will ensure that you consider every aspect and thereby enjoy healthier and more realistic relationships with your fellow workers.

6

difficult customers – how do I deal with them?

Customers are the 'oil in the engine' that makes business run – whether selling goods or services there is some form of customer interaction, either external or internal to your business. Over recent years we have moved closer to a customer care culture, impacting on customer behaviour in both positive and negative ways. Of course customers are essential but there is a balance to be struck between what is reasonable or not. The economic situation at any point may also have an impact on your customer procedures.

The customer relationship is not just about selling goods, there is plenty of useful information that can be gleaned from customers, and techniques for turning negative situations into positive ones that grow your business further. The customer culture is here to stay and therefore difficult customers need to be considered as an intrinsic part of your business, from whom you can glean so much.

All businesses need customers. Somebody somewhere has to buy something, whether that be tangible goods and products or services. The customer is immensely important to the transaction and in large organisations, where people deal only with numbers, it may seem that no one actually sees the customer – but that does not mean that they are not there. Businesses need customers to operate and whatever your role, you need to be aware of their impact. Customer fickleness is also legendary and a lack of awareness of how your customers think, together with future trends, could lead you to be seriously out of step.

The customer relationship, however, does not have to be one-sided. Customers can be rude, difficult and downright annoying but you both need each other – or do you? If you are having serious problems with a customer, you might be tempted to think about the balance to which you both contribute to the transaction, and let a lower payback go. For example, a customer who buys TVs in blocks of 50 or more for the rooms in his chain of hotels has a problem that needs resolving. You will surely be very keen to help him out as you know for sure he will be back again if you can assure him of a swift resolution. But what about the lady who buys one TV and has a problem? Do you treat her the same or do you think, 'Well she is a small spender, so let her complain, I don't have to deal with it if I don't want to.' Let's see what happens when we ignore her and also fail to be aware of the multiplier effect.

The Accumulator Effect

Now let us assume this TV was priced at £200, and you told the customer that you were not going to deal with the problem.

The lady in the example above goes to a family dinner that night with four other people who were naturally enquiring about her day. Of course, she tells them about her problem, warning them away from ever doing business with you. Those four people represent $4 \times £200 = £800$ in possible lost revenue.

Now imagine that the following day, they each tell another four people about their relative's problem, which would represent 16 × £200 = £3200 of possible lost revenue. So far, that is £4000 of possible lost revenue from not dealing with one person effectively.

I know what you are thinking, that probably those people were not all going to buy a £200 TV in the near future. Well, maybe some of them were, and maybe some were going to spend more – in fact it is likely that, were any of these people to buy a TV at all in the future, they would not now 'risk' buying from you; after all, there are so many other places to choose from. It is also highly likely that they would pass this story on to many more people than in the example – the story might even make it into the local papers!

The accumulator effect can be hugely damaging – if you are still not convinced consider the case of a certain famous jewellers and how their business all but disappeared overnight following flippant comments by one of the directors, regarding the quality of their goods, on national television.

There is also the issue of the internal customer. When organisations depend on internal divisions to provide a service to each other, this necessarily creates the concept of internal customisation. By taking the view that everyone is the customer of someone else – even within the business – processes can become more streamlined and there is more of a sense of everyone contributing towards the whole.

Being prompt in identifying the real issues

If you are a customer of goods or services that do not meet your personal idea of quality, what do you do? You would probably think that you ought to complain or get your feelings across to someone because you want something done about the situation.

You may also think that perhaps someone should be responsible for this error. The key point here is that you would want someone to:

* acknowledge the situation, and then hopefully
* take some form of action.

This is where so many people go wrong in customer care. The first step can take but a few minutes but the second step – the action – may take longer.

An initial fast and efficient way of dealing with customer issues can prevent many long-term problems. When dealing with customer issues at the initial stage the most important aspects are being able to:

* hear the problem
* take effective notes
* acknowledge the feelings behind the problem
* undertake some form of action
* follow through.

Let's just look at that in more detail.

Hear the problem

This means actually paying close attention to what the issue is. What is essential is that you listen carefully and extract the details while homing in on the real issue under dispute. Also try to ascertain what the customer actually wants as recompense. It is helpful to know whether someone complaining about a malfunctioning camera is asking for a repair, a replacement, or recompense for the whole wedding that was ruined due to the lack of photographs.

Take effective notes

These will help you, or whoever is dealing with the problem, later on.

In essence:

* What is the situation?
* Where did it happen (or where is the item)?
* Why did this happen or come about?
* How did it happen?

* When did it happen?
* To whom did it happen?

Acknowledge the feelings behind the problem

The problem is not the only problem, when it comes to customer care. The other issue is how the customer is feeling about the situation. Two customers may react totally differently to a similar situation. For one, a broken product is a mere inconvenience and, for another, the end of the world.

Undertake some form of action

This is not the final action or outcome, this is something you can do NOW to help this person. Summarise the situation as you now understand it, tell the customer that you have made notes, who they will be passed on to, and when they can expect to be contacted and the method. Immediately treat this as urgent to contain the problem as being the initial problem and not some escalated version of the situation, and take the next step as necessary, whether that be seeking help or passing it on to another relevant person.

Follow through

Nothing will annoy a customer more than if promises are not held. This will add even more fire to their already burning anger and, for many, a lack of follow through will be the final straw. Keep them informed and updated on every stage of the process, and there is a good chance you will win them back.

It is unrealistic to believe that there will not be some faults with all the products and services that we use in our lifetime, but the way in which these are handled lead either to customers turning their backs or to customer loyalty.

Is the problem situational or personal?

However, what happens when the problem is not about a product but a person? This adds a new dimension to dealing with the issue at large. It may be that the customer is complaining about a sales assistant, someone on the telephone, the person who is handling their complaint, or possibly even yourself.

In a situation where there is a complaint about a person, it is important then, to separate:

* the message given
* the way in which it was delivered
* the person who delivered the message.

The message given

This could be that your organisation's procedures do not marry up with the expectations of the customer. For example, you may have a policy that any complaint that is received outside of the warranty period is not to be dealt with. If this is the case, a complaint against a customer telephone officer may be an underlying annoyance about your policy rather than the person themselves.

The way in which it was delivered

All staff dealing with customer complaints should undergo some form of customer care training. There are different ways of conveying a message and the tone and phrase in which a message is given can have a great effect on how it is received.

The person who delivered the message

There may be occasions when the complaint does come down to the individual. Possible causes of complaint could be leaving customers hanging on, not following procedures, or not having any respect for the customer at all; any of this may point to poor business behaviour. If you find this to be the problem, you will need to speak with the individual and decide the next course of action. In the short term, and to help the customer, it would be pertinent to appoint another person to deal with the original complaint, or deal with it yourself. In the longer term you have a performance issue that you now need to address with the staff member, and this may mean you liaising with another manager if they are not in your department or team.

Are there things you can put right?

When it comes to dealing with difficult customers, you need to be very sure of your mandate. What exactly can you offer customers and what is out of bounds? For example, you may be able to offer them money in compensation, but it might have to come directly out of your own budget! Or perhaps every compensation, however small, has to be discussed and signed off by senior management.

In some organisations, and many parts of local government, monetary awards to external customers are certainly discouraged. In the retail sector vouchers are often given, ensuring that the customer has to come back to spend them, and hopefully has a better experience next time. It is certainly worth finding out what the difficult customer thinks is sufficient recompense. If they are making themselves difficult because they want a monetary payout and that is not your policy, it is worth stating that upfront, as that may well end the situation.

What are your grounds for negotiation?

So, you have established that your customer has some grounds for complaint but you have not agreed to the extent of the problem or any further action. At the moment the customer is angry. How can you turn this situation around? Well, you could move immediately to settlement of the issue (in whatever way you decide), but then you lose a big opportunity to engage with the customer and perhaps win back their trust and future business. In this situation you are in a position to negotiate, and the negotiation is again not just about the terms of settlement but about engaging the customer and hopefully winning them over for the future.

There are four stages to negotiation:
* **Preparation** – find out all you can about the situation, how long it has been going on for, what has been written/said, this customer's track record, what they want to achieve.
* **Discuss** – other staff may have been involved in this situation before you stepped in.
* **Propose** – decide either independently or with your organisation what the parameters of any award may be (at this stage there may be minimum and maximum amounts).
* **Bargain** – handle the negotiation with the customer, aiming for a win–win situation if possible.

In any situation, there are four possible outcomes from a negotiation:
* **Win–lose** – this is where you win on the negotiation but at the expense of the other person. For example, 'No we will not offer you anything and suggest you shop elsewhere in the future.'
* **Lose–win** – this is where you lose but the customer wins. For example, 'I am sorry that the spillage spoilt your clothes. We will pay for the dry cleaning bill and also offer you a year's free dining at any of our restaurants.'
* **Lose–lose** – in this outcome you are both losers. For example, 'I will replace everything at my own personal cost and I fully understand that you don't want to shop here again.'
* **Win–win** – this is the ideal outcome, where you both get something out of the negotiation, for example, 'We will replace the product, including postage, and send you a voucher for 10 per cent discount on your next purchase. We are sorry that this mistake has happened and hope that you will remain a good customer of Busy PCs.'

In the win–win situation you will see that the customer achieved their result – a speedy resolution – and also came away with a voucher, which has cost Busy PCs very little in actual money as the discount will come off their mark-up. The customer feels they have something extra and the voucher means that they are more inclined to go back there in the future, if only to browse what to possibly spend it on.

A successful negotiation can actually win you customer support in the long run and once again who will these one-time difficult people tell? Other people, of course, and you will have turned a negative customer situation into a positive one.

Conclusion

When you are dealing with difficult customers you need to decide initially whether there is a case for their annoyance. If there is, then the fault lies with your organisation and you need to speak with senior management about improving your quality and systems. If it really is the customer who is difficult, consider first how much their business is worth to you, and whether, rather than pushing them away, you should really be involving them more.

7

difficult suppliers — how should I deal with them?

Although we discussed customers in the previous chapter, suppliers are also customers and form part of the sales chain. Every business needs to consider its suppliers regularly to ensure that it is benefiting from the most appropriate supply solution – for some this might mean the lowest prices but for another it might be generous credit terms. Whatever criteria your business is measuring their suppliers against, it is crucial to convey this information and then work together to ensure the relationship continues.

From time to time it may be that a supplier is forced to change its focus or practices, in the same way that you might change your customer sales strategy, depending on the market. It is important, therefore, that we look at any difficulty from that perspective. It pays to remember that understanding your suppliers and being honest with them can ensure you a long and fruitful relationship.

Suppliers do not just supply products or materials, they are also all your consultants, trainers, advisers, professional bodies – in fact anyone who provides you with information, goods and services. When a supplier falters in their provision there are a number of options available to you and it is quite clear that, if the goods and services are not being provided, you must either find another way of obtaining them – or redesign your processes so that you no longer need them. But what if the supplier is just being difficult? What happens if they withhold payment, start to impose new penalties in contracts that are not beneficial to you, or start to provide for a competitor? Where do you stand then and how do you deal with them?

Let's look at the background to this. The supply and demand chain is a fine balance between running a successful business and not having the materials to work with. It is rather like a web where everyone has their part. One tear in that web can affect the whole structure and although it may not bring it down completely, it becomes more fragile and unbalanced until the tear is repaired again. This fragility helps no one and companies can be brought down by relatively minor 'tears' to their web.

For this reason it is not uncommon for companies to even buy out their supplier if the supplier gets into financial difficulties. Businesses depend on other businesses for their survival and the relationship between them is a finely balanced one.

Getting it in perspective

Problems with suppliers can become very emotional and therefore it is a good idea to put the whole situation into perspective before rushing in with an ill-judged solution. Decisions made on the hoof often cause other problems later on.

Let's look at a more analytical or process approach. You are having a problem with one of your suppliers:

1 Firstly, is this a situation caused by you (or your organisation)? This initial question is important not just to judge who is the aggrieved party, but if it is something you have caused, you may be able to put things right again. For example, you may

have changed your payment dates and that now makes it impossible for your supplier to buy their raw material in time to produce their order for you. If that is the case, then you may be able to move it back to the original dates again. If so, problem solved!

2 Secondly, is this a one-off problem, or an ongoing one? You need to know whether you are dealing with a 'for now' situation or one that will keep recurring. For a one-off situation or problem you might put in emergency measures or even pay a little more to get you out of a fix but this is not sustainable. For example, the guy who supplies your web-presence (looking after your website and online advertising) breaks his arm in an accident. You are desperate to get a new offer out to your internet customers and so you start to look at who else could do it. All other suppliers of this service want to charge you at least twice the cost because you are not offering a long-term contract, but you may reason that this is a one-off situation, and as your original guy will be back at work as soon as he can be, you will pay and take the hit of the extra costs (and appreciate him more in the future)! In other words, it is worth throwing some money at this one because the problem is a short-term one.

3 Thirdly, in which part of your business is the problem? Not all areas of your business are equal. Some products or services are more key to business success than others, some yield more profit, and this may affect how you react to a supplier problem. For example, if an area is key to your business success you will view any supplier problem as having critical effect, whereas if the business area has much less impact on bottom-line performance, you may decide to deal with the problem differently.

Now that you have these three pieces of analytical information, you should be more able to react in an appropriate manner based on solid information rather than gut feelings and panic. If it is to be the end of the relationship, at least it will be based on logical thinking and some solid facts, rather than gut instinct clouded by emotion.

Looking at your previous relationship

Thousands of new businesses open up worldwide every year. If you look to the international market the number is mind boggling – and they are all after your business. Some are willing to offer generous incentives to new customers, and others (such as fuel companies) are even willing to handle the switch-over for you. If you have been dealing with the same supplier for years because it is either too difficult to change or you think no one else out there offers the same, it is time to look again.

Every so often it pays to undertake a proper supplier analysis. This means looking not only at your suppliers but who else is out there and what would be the implications of changing supplier. Questions you need to ask are:

* **Who are your suppliers?** Think about your business as a whole. Who supplies everything from the staples to the key components? Who provides you with temporary staff? Who supplies your stationery? How long have you been trading with them, and what is their track record? Are you buying from two suppliers where one could suffice (and you may be able to negotiate a greater discount)? Also note how you access your supplies. You may pay more to a local supplier but save on transportation or postage costs.

* **Who else is out there?** Some items such as stationery have plentiful competition but others such as a factory floor sweeping machine will have very few. Although rare, in some instances your supplier may be the only one. Again, look at the geographical issue. Certain goods are cheaper to buy from different parts of the country, or even abroad, perhaps where wages are lower and housing costs less. The internet is a good place to start to find out who is offering what but also consider asking local Business Links and Chamber of Commerce and also consult trade directories.

* **What would be the implications of change?** You need to think broadly on this one. Closing an account with a supplier in one department could cause another to lose their 'goodwill

discount' because the supplier viewed the two accounts as the total commitment from your business. Business is more than money, and you run the risk of spoiling a helpful relationship, if you don't consider every implication. You need to see the bigger picture before you make such an important decision.

Now for the emotional angle. Be honest, over the past few years, has the relationship been good? What emotions are tied up in the relationship? Are the suppliers personal friends of yours or even family members? Do you have a reciprocal arrangement whereby your business helps them out? If you answered yes to any of these questions, you may find that it is not so easy to change because you have a psychological contract that is greater than just paper and ink.

This exercise was focused on closely analysing your situation and not necessarily moving on from regular suppliers who may be difficult. You just need to know all the facts to make sure you begin to think about whether they are still the right suppliers for the future.

Are they right for your future?

Staying with the same supplier can be cosy, and what if they do become a little difficult? Your company has always traded with them, they don't mean it. There is no point looking around because they are all the same, aren't they? If we all thought like this no new businesses would ever get off the ground. All businesses have had to change over the years, and that includes giving you good customer service.

Customer service, as a phenomenon, came from the US and has now permeated most UK businesses. However, the trends have not stopped there and there are a plethora of new values you need to consider when selecting a new supplier, or electing to remain with your exisiting supplier. In brief:

* **Corporate responsibility** This means an organisation demonstrating that it understands the responsibility it has for intruding into our lives. It could be that, for every 1000 boxes of paper that it sells, it will donate £100 to a neighbourhood project. Many companies now have their own charities that they openly support.

* **Ethical trading** This means that a company will only trade with companies that are ethical and have certain morals and values. The pay their staff a fair amount for the work they do and they contribute to local communities and society.
* **Environmentally friendly** This means that they use materials in all areas of their work that are just that – environmentally friendly. These materials are kinder to the environment and will largely be recyclable. Environmentally friendly will also cover any recycling policy the company may have.
* **Sustainability** This refers to whether the business will be around in a few year's time. Businesses need to be able to survive in bad years as well as good, and if the company has thought about sustainability it will have built in a number of measures so that it can continue to survive through the most difficult of times.
* **Investors in People (IiP) and people care** This is concerned with how staff are treated and kept informed.

Why are we mentioning these new trends? Many suppliers are now being asked to demonstrate that they meet most of these criteria. It is no longer enough to buy from a supplier because they produce just what you want; they also need to demonstrate that they are able to supply these items from within a structure that is fair, ethical and environmentally sound.

Building new supplier relationships that last

When you move into new relationships with suppliers there will always be the honeymoon period when you are both working to help each other. You are keen to get someone on board and get settled with a regular supplier, they are pleased to have a new customer and want to show their appreciation. It is a great time, but it won't necessarily last. It is not unusual to experience trouble at some point in any supplier/buyer relationship, but the degree to which that trouble rocks your foundations depends on how you have built your relationship.

Start by looking at any contracts and query those clauses that you do not understand, do not think are fair, or do not agree with. Contracts are negotiable: just because they say, 'payment in 10 days' does not mean that you cannot challenge this and negotiate an extension to something you may find more reasonable, but of course you need to do this at the beginning of the relationship.

As much as possible, deal in a transparent way. This means not hiding any aspects of the business from your supplier. Trust is essential in any relationship and if they suspect you are hiding something, you may find it difficult to recover.

It is very difficult to start any relationship by assuming problems, but in the same way that a prenuptial agreement is becoming very fashionable, you need to think through what would happen if things went awry. It is very similar to producing a risk analysis that you might easily do on any project, but might not consider for any new supplier.

Build your supplier relationships on win–win wherever you can. Between you there is a great deal of power and opportunity. Some organisations openly recommend each other, and that is always good for business. Seize this opportunity to help each other and you could both be the better for it.

Conclusion

Dealing with suppliers is more than a daily transaction. There can be more than the contract on the table; there can also be a psychological contract in operation. At times you may feed off each other's customers and business, deals may be done and business shared, but the essential company–supplier relationship has to remain.

Where there are difficult relationships of any kind, this can add extra pressure with the opportunity for misunderstanding and the generation of problems. If you need to work together effectively consider a contract that specifies any nuances and stipulates how you will handle your relationship.

You can then consider whether the suppliers you have really do help your business and add value to it, or devalue you by association.

8

how do I deal with difficult people from other cultures and countries?

The world is becoming increasingly smaller and many contracts are now handled by organisations and people in other countries. This results in many different cultures working together. This initial mix of culture can be based on suspicion or on intrigue, but the results will be different in each interaction. Base your thoughts on suspicion and your lack of trust will be conveyed to the other person and treated accordingly. However, if you are able to enter with an open mind, full of genuine interest, then you may have a very different response.

We need to look at whether the difficulty is a cultural one or whether there are other factors at play. This chapter will help you think through the issues involved in working and communicating with people from other cultures and countries and provide you with some helpful ideas that may make all the difference in your future interactions.

The world is now a very small place. In the past, an organisation running an office abroad would have seemed glamorous in the extreme but now many organisations have international offices. Staff from overseas offices will spend some time with your company and a lack of communication and understanding could be embarrassing for all.

Not only might your organisation have international offices but it may deal extensively with other nationalities and could possibly have outsourced many of its services to other nations. Years ago, customer service and the manufacturing of your goods would have been considered far too crucial to the front end of business to be passed outside of the organisation, let alone out of the country. However, the international market, increase in technology and the insistence of the customer to drive down costs mean that these two functions alone often operate out of say, China or India. If they are operating from there, you will need staff to liaise and ensure their contract is working effectively.

The role of diversity in society

To keep pace with the changes in society (and in some instances to promote those changes) specific laws have been put in place that make it illegal to discriminate against anyone in a number of key areas – race and religion being just two of them.

Diversity simply means difference and promoting it acknowledges that so many different people can contribute to life and the working economy. Working with diversity challenges you to consider the benefits of having staff with different backgrounds, cultures and ideas, and to think of the extra value they can bring to the organisation. If you wanted to expand your business overseas you would need specialist advice and perhaps an interpreter to help you set up your business. If you already had employees of that nationality, who are able to help you, the process could be a whole lot easier and you would avoid having to employ consultants and translators.

Health warning! Note that each country has its own legal system, and equality legislation, for example, will vary. If you have offices abroad or travel, you need to research the laws pertaining to that area/state/country.

Stereotypes

When we think of different cultures we often use stereotypes. These are templates that we use to categorise and make assumptions, for example, red-haired people have hot, fiery tempers. If you are reading this book because of some of the difficult people in your life you will know that lots of people have fiery tempers, it is not limited to people with red hair, and so the stereotype is quite unfair. Not only can it be wrong, it can also be very hurtful to the individual. However, stereotypes are not always the 'bad guys' people make them out to be and can have their use – if they are tempered with intelligence and common sense.

Stereotypes, then, can be useful in grouping ideas together but they are limited in their reality. Put into a cultural context, you may approach someone who looks visibly Asian with one set of stereotyped thoughts and assumptions only to find out that they have very Western ideas and their family have lived in this country for several generations.

Does this mean that we should ignore all stereotypical thoughts then? I would say not. These groupings can be extremely useful in certain circumstances: it is our blind reliance on them that is the problem. Taken delicately as only ever providing a few tentative ideas about the person, they can be most helpful.

To demonstrate how stereotypes can be helpful, let's look at this practically. Your company is opening up an office in Spain and therefore you go to discuss the arrangements with someone called Juan Carlos. You are met by a man who appears typically Spanish, and you decide to greet him with a typical greeting 'Hola. Buenos días'. He seems *hugely* pleased that you greeted him thus and it augers well for a good working relationship. This worked well because in your brain you assumed that someone with that name, dark colouring, in Spain, coming forward to greet you, just might be Spanish.

Where it does not work well is when you return home and are told that the company is also opening an office in Japan. Later that day you see someone in the corridor who you have not seen before, and he has distinct Eastern looks. You make the assumption that he must be here to discuss the new office in Japan, and so try to greet him with a bow, which he finds hilarious because he is actually the new IT guy from Bexley.

The difference between the two scenarios is the actions and assumptions we make. Our brain does a quick probability test to ascertain the most likely scenario, enabling us to act on it. In the first scenario the probability was high that the man was indeed your Spanish representative. In the second scenario you made the same assumptions but came up with the wrong answer. To make matters worse you are sure that the IT guy will never forget this and you will be laughed at by everyone as he shares his story throughout the company.

Stereotypes and assumptions can be really useful but you need to cross-check the data to make sure it is accurate.

Difficult people or simply different cultures?

Usually when we say someone is being difficult it is because they are not performing in the way we want and expect them to. In many instances people are not actively trying to be difficult, but interpret your words in a different way – in essence 'You say potato and I say patattha'. This leads to a mismatch in understanding. Some cultures operate in a very laid back manner. Asking them to respond quickly is simply not on their radar. They are not being difficult – just different.

It would take a vast knowledge of the world to avoid all these pitfalls, and again you have to be very wary of stereotypes, as there is always an exception to every rule. However, when a problem arises with someone from another culture you have to consider whether it is really a behavioural problem or a cultural one.

The other point to consider is that there is a danger that we are always looking for difference. We may be from different cultures but do we both like music, films, eating out, and so forth? When we make friendships we are doing this instinctively. Every friendship we have is made through shared experience – such as finding out we used to live in the same town or were both only children – and therefore finding commonality is far more positive. As a team activity, ask staff to find commonalities. It will be bonding for relationships and you will find that people are not all as completely different as we may suppose.

Effective communication and understanding

If you need to visit or work in another country, you will have to learn the nuances of that country. For example, hand gestures can mean very different things wherever you go. If this is the case, I would recommend that you go on a specialist cultural initiation course so that you do not offend any business contacts or clients. Most people are forgiving to a point but it shows a lack of preparation and understanding to blunder your way in and insult people, no matter what your excuse.

Another alternative is to find a national or expert to guide you gently through any negotiations, and even translate for you.

The international team

In terms of business development international teams have the world at their fingertips, and we may be seeing more and more of these around in the future. The world market is huge and trading between countries is the highest it has ever been. In business as in all things there always has been the danger that we only see what is on our own horizon and ignore that beyond. How many of us truly think globally when we consider options for our business? But there are bigger markets out there than we ever dreamed possible. For example the Bollywood film industry far outsells anything Hollywood has to offer. Building diversity into teams can enable more opportunities for tapping into international markets. If you have people of different cultures in your team and are not capitalising on the benefits of this, then you just might be missing a trick.

If you are already working in a diverse team, or have connections with another team abroad, the very essence of being a member of that team may also be very different. In some cultures the team socialise and lunch together, in others it is strictly business between set hours, and then home. In some Mediterranean countries it is the norm to have longer midday breaks and a late afternoon return to work. This can cause confusion if you are not aware and are trying to contact them between twelve o'clock and two. In the same way that some nationalities greet each other with a kiss, some teams are more intimate with each other than others. Some countries, for example, the UK, are known for their reserve but if you visit teams in other countries don't be surprised to see them acting as if they are family members. If you are not sure, err on the polite but more formal side, and only when someone has you in a bear-hug feel free to reciprocate.

Conclusion

Working with people of different nationalities can be very interesting. Behind every action and intention there may be a different set of values, rules and thought processes, which in itself is very enlightening and educational.

When looking to work with people of different nationalities take note of stereotypes but do not be led by them. Try to kill as many assumptions as possible and maintain an open mind – even within a different culture there will be further difference and freedom of thought. It might be helpful to remember some generalisations as long as you maintain an open mind to anomalies.

Try to find out as much about people as possible including their practices and religion. This will tell you much about how to behave and what is expected (including dress code). If visiting a team in their own country, try to learn, at the very least, a polite greeting to demonstrate that you have made the effort, and don't forget to smile.

how do I cope if I am the one being difficult?

'Mirror, mirror on the wall, who is the most difficult of all?' – surely it can't be the person staring back at you, can it? It is never comfortable to think that any difficult situation with another person may be grounded in our own behaviour but unfortunately that is sometimes the case. We all have the potential to act and be difficult in certain circumstances, creating the very situation and behaviours that we are now accusing others of undertaking to annoy us. Most of our reactions take place before we are even aware of them, but when the situation is tricky, a greater awareness could provide an insight to the response we receive.

Self analysis is not for everyone but if you are truly looking to tackle a situation with another person, it might very well be worth starting closer to home before shifting all the blame onto the other person.

Throughout this book we have discussed many types of people and difficult situations and I have mentioned several times about the importance of the dynamic – the fact that between two people there exists a third communication conundrum that appears to work all by itself. My reason for mentioning this again is that, when we look to the possibility of difficult behaviour in others, we also have to look to ourselves. Taking the attitude of problems being 'out there' or always grounded in other people is not sustainable, especially if you seem to be experiencing a whole load of problems with everyone. Have you considered that perhaps the problem is closer to home? If you have never had any management or skills training you may not be dealing with people in the most effective way, and you may have to face up to the fact that it may be your behaviour that is triggering or at least contributing towards the problem.

Remember: I have said this before but it bears being repeated here. You cannot enforce change on other people, you can only change your own behaviour, thoughts and beliefs. You can model the behaviour you want to see in others, and encourage them to follow, but you cannot change them – they have to want to change themselves.

So, if the problem, perhaps, is more to do with you, how would you know? Do you have regular feedback sessions with your managers? Perhaps they have spoken to you or hinted even that your handling of the team or certain situations is not good? Have you had outbursts with staff where they felt able to be honest about your style?

Facing up to your prejudices and assumptions

Now, before we all put our hands up and say, 'Not me', let's get one thing straight – we all hold prejudices and make assumptions. The previous chapter looked at prejudice. The emphasis there was on cultural prejudice but prejudice can take any form and we all have it.

Where do prejudices come from?

Prejudice may be defined as 'where a judgement or decision is made on the basis of little or no factual information' and comes from our life experiences or what we have been told. Notice the emphasis on the lack of factual information. Prejudices are not rational, logical knowledge, they are untested falsehoods that can create serious limitations and blockages to our thinking. Our parents will be responsible for creating some of our deepest prejudices, quite possibly for the best of reasons. Whenever they told you to keep away from certain types of people, to keep you safe, they were setting up prejudice, but before we lay every blame on our parents, we are more than capable of creating or absorbing many others throughout our life, through school and into adulthood. People do form natural groups, such as those based on nationalities, hobbies or physical appearance, and not seeing them as individuals may be extremely limiting. Discrimination legislation is there to protect minority groups from this type of treatment and therefore you need to be aware of it and the impact it can make on your business.

Why do we make assumptions?

Assumptions are also part of our short-cutting mechanism. To enable us to make fast decisions, we need to assume certain aspects when the correct data is not to hand. This can be very sensible, for example, all things glowing red are possibly very hot and so we would not naturally reach out and put our hand on a glowing metal plate, just to test it. However, assumptions again can also be very limiting, such as assuming that all mothers of children are not interested in pursuing a career, when in fact as many women with children want to pursue careers as those without children do. In this example, a stereotype (of a classic mother – perhaps modelled on your own mother) has become an assumption (she won't want career progression, she is too busy bringing up her children) and the assumption may form the basis of prejudice if you then decide not to allow this person to go on any courses or to move ahead in her career just because of your opinion of her. Any assumption must always be checked out, as this person may be waiting in the wings to lead your next winning team, but if they are never offered any opportunity, they may leave in disgust (or in an extreme situation, take you to court for discrimination).

That critical millisecond called 'choice'

We have already covered the concept that you cannot make anyone change – only make them aware of the problem, model good behaviour, influence and support. Everyone has the choice as to whether to change and that also refers to you. When people tell me, 'I can't help the way I am, I just have a short temper', or 'I don't know why I get so irritated by them, I just can't stop myself', they are ignoring the one thing we have that makes us very different from all other animals on the planet – choice.

You have far more control over your behaviour than you think. There is a critical millisecond called 'choice' where you can think before you act. The same person will tell me that they feel helpless if they shout at a junior member of staff when they make an error, and yet withhold that behaviour if the person who made the error was a senior manager. Since shouting at staff senior to yourself is usually career limiting, they have decided in that critical millisecond to hold their tongue. So they are not really a hostage to their actions all the time, and control is nearer than you may think.

Don't be a captive to your emotions, don't hide behind 'I can't change' or 'This is who I am' if that behaviour is inappropriate. We can all change, we just need to give ourselves permission to do so and ensure the change is for the better.

Practising positive intent and modelling behaviour

We are all modelling a set of behaviours that tells the world about us and how we operate, and this can quickly become a blueprint for how the team operates. We are all very good at picking up on body language and verbal interactions, assimilating the information and incorporating it into our own. (Think of how children very quickly learn not only the mannerisms of their parents, but also their weak areas.) Modelling behaviour demonstrates to others what we find acceptable and how we would like to be treated.

The next step on from this is to demonstrate positive intent. This is a term borrowed from the counselling sector and is used to describe how an individual forms a mindset that assumes that, no matter what the other person has said or done, it has been done with positive intent. On the whole, most people are good and do things for the right reasons, even when the results turn out wrong! By blasting off about a failed outcome you run the risk of causing them upset, humiliation and destroying any long-term relationship you may have created. Now, instead of getting angry immediately, assume the mindset that, whatever the outcome, the person was probably acting in the best interests of the team/project at that time. Notice how the situation suddenly becomes different. For a start it is not about them but about the outcome and possibly, just possibly, it was not actually their fault. By creating a mindset of positive intent we are able to put these mistakes into perspective and react to them on a more authentic, and reasonable, level.

Finding the right immediate response

When someone brings a problem to you, the temptation may be to react emotionally. If that is the right response, then there is time for that later. What we need to do is have an appropriate immediate response that is blame free (after all you don't yet know the facts), and enables you to investigate the situation without destroying everyone in your wake. It is far easier to deal with this rationally at the time, than have to go back and admit you were either wrong or that you acted inappropriately.

The answer is surprisingly easy but may not be your first choice of response, and for this reason it needs practice. The next time someone approaches you with some 'disaster' or mistake, keep calm. Ask them to explain the situation fully, as they see it, and make some notes. At this point, hopefully, the fact that they are talking and you are writing will enable you to keep a rein on any potential outburst. Put all of your remaining energy into active listening rather than speaking. When they have finished, unless very urgent action is required, say something like, 'I need to look into this a little more. Can you come back in half an hour when we can discuss the situation more fully.' If the matter is exceptionally urgent, then try taking three, discreet, deep 'stomach breaths' before replying. This tiny intervention will enable you to insert a break into your normal reaction and immediately give you the choice to take control in a proactive manner, allowing you to reply in a more appropriate way.

Gaining a greater understanding of yourself

Realising that we all have shortcomings is an important part of our adult development, and we can only do this through gaining a greater understanding of our personalities and our motivations. When we face up to certain aspects about ourselves we have the building blocks to move forward and become the people we want to be.

Greater understanding of yourself can start with a thorough understanding of how others see you. Ever done a 360? (And no, I don't mean a spin on the spot!) 360 degree feedback is a mechanism whereby the same questionnaire is handed out to:

* those in a role above you
* those junior to your role
* a number of colleagues (both external and internal)

This puts you at the very centre of the process and invites everyone around you, hence the term '360 degree', to provide an opinion on your behaviour and competence. This information is then fed back to you via a facilitator.

The resulting information can then be measured statistically against your own opinion of you. 360 degree feedback mechanisms are very powerful when considering your own behaviour and how it impacts on others with whom you work every day. If others view your behaviours and skills lower than you do yourself, you could have a problem whereby you consider yourself far superior to the reality. If you score yourself much lower than others do, it could reveal a serious lack of self-confidence or false modesty. What you are looking for here is an honest summary of your behaviours, and from the feedback you can begin to see how these can be adjusted to work with others more effectively.

When you have your overall report you need to spend some time considering how you feel about the outcome. Do you feel it is a fair representation of you? Is it how you would like to be perceived? Does your style fit with the culture and the way your organisation sees itself in the future? It can be very hard to accept that others find us annoying, a problem or difficult in any way to work with. Defence mechanisms kick in whenever we don't want to hear the message. However, if we do not accept the feedback, then we cannot move forward and make changes. How you accept your feedback will determine your future. If you decide that there is room for improvement then you can work with your direct manager to put forward a plan for development.

Learning and accepting is the key principle – without that you will never fulfil your potential.

Conclusion

Sometimes the problem is us and there is no escaping that fact, however uncomfortable it may be. There are certain things that we can do to get good feedback on our behaviour and then to implement some changes that will benefit not only the team or staff group, but also challenge some of our ingrained prejudices and assumptions.

10

how can I manage conflicting team members?

Over the past twenty years business has seen a move away from the mechanical aspect of managing and towards people management, including team management. It is accepted that people achieve more when working in a team environment, but that means managing your team while helping everyone to get the most from the dynamic. In essence you need to be able to both motivate, mediate, challenge and support. Adding to this complication is that teams should be diverse and lively – after all, that is where the creativity comes from!

However balancing this while also ensuring that the job gets done can be tricky as, on occasions, what causes the conflict can also be the source of competitive drive. If you are to be not just an effective team leader but heading up a high performing team, you will need the skills to manage individuals as well as the dynamic between them.

Wherever people are together there is conflict. One person believes that they are not getting the same levels of attention or opportunities as someone else. Another person thinks they are overworked while another thinks they are not trusted. People on their own can be difficult but put them in a team and the web becomes far more intricate because the dynamics create a whole new level of volatility. When you work with difficult people in a team you are not just working with individuals – you are also working with something that is going on between individuals.

Three key things that should under pin all other factors are:

1 You are the manager. It sounds obvious but if you are the team leader or manager you have been put in that place to do just that – manage. Therefore there has to be a point at which you say 'I am going to do something about this', and you have the authority to do so.

2 This is a work situation. We may be able to choose who we marry or live with but we cannot necessarily select who we work with – nor should we. Team workers should be selected for what skills, knowledge and attributes they bring to the team and the work – not the skills, knowledge and attributes you would like in a best friend. Work situations demand that the focus is not necessarily on having fun, it is on achieving goals. People at work do not have to be friends, but they do need to be professional, and are in fact paid to be so.

3 Teams do not need to share everything. If you wish to address an issue with one person, never be tempted to take them to task openly. Everyone deserves respect and should be treated accordingly. Always tackle a behaviour or performance issue in private, away from the rest of the team.

Teams cannot always get along but every member should make an attempt at being professional and this can be noted through their regular one-to-one meetings or appraisals.

Keeping an eye on the balance

When we select team members we want a good mix of skills, knowledge and attitude, however most recruitment processes look at the two former attributes and perform very little testing on the latter. The consequence of this is that we have teams who should be great performers and cover every angle of a project plan, but actually don't get on or display any attempt at trying.

Seemingly petty issues will arise and you will need to keep some semblance of order, if only to ensure the work actually does get done. However, not all teams are full of 'characters', some seemingly exist in perpetual harmony. Is this what we should be aiming for? Not necessarily. Balance is needed in all teams. The danger with too much harmony is that no one is asking the challenging questions. A team of 'Yes' people will still be nodding their approval as they drive off the edge of the cliff!

What you need is a balance of different types of people who have a spread of skills. At this point you may be excused for thinking, 'Well, it's OK if I can select my dream team for balance on all levels, but I inherited my people. They were not chosen so much as handed over.' Actually, this is not as problematic as you may have thought. If it is any consolation, even 'designer' teams have problems because people change. As a result of things happening in our lives none of us are the people we were last week. I may have felt pretty calm yesterday but stressed up to my eyeballs today. Envying a 'designer' team is a hollow emotion. Think about the team you have. If they are problematic, at least you know about it. You know the characters and the more they perform to type the more you can make assumptions about their reactions. When you know where the likely problem areas are, you can begin to create strategies to deal with them.

Now you are seeing the team for what they are, a varied group who have a wide number of talents, albeit in different areas. Their talents need bringing out and acknowledging. Everyone has something to give to the team or an effect upon it. For example, even the quietest person may have a calming effect when there is conflict. Accept that they will have conflicting ideas and upset each other with their different ways of operating. You will need all your higher level skills to work with them – life is nothing if not a challenge – and anyone who does not like people has no business managing teams.

Think also about your own style and balance. You must treat everyone equally. This does not necessarily mean that people should always be handled in the same way, but they must have equal treatment and opportunities. The way in which you handle the team will have far more effect on them than you realise and your balanced approach will help to stabilise the team.

You may still want to make some changes. However, bear in mind that change is easier to implement if you acknowledge to everyone that there are some positives in what they are currently doing, but that you now need to tweak this to accommodate new ways of working. It is easier for the team to change if they are not told that their behaviour is untenable, poor, difficult, unhelpful – or any of the other negatives you may have used in the past.

Divorcing the situation from the emotion

In every altercation there will be a great deal of emotion. Emotion is great at helping us to express our hurt to other parties and it also helps us to free ourselves from pent-up frustrations that would make us ill were we to internalise them. Emotion, then, has very useful functions, but it is not effective when it clouds thinking processes and prevents rational decision making. Telling someone in distress, 'Don't be so emotional', is not very helpful either at the time or in the long term.

Dealing with emotions in the team needs a gentle touch. There is no point in expecting an emotional person to act rationally so shelve any solid actions for now. Let's deal instead with the emotions and try to get those under control. When people are upset it is understandable that they may want to cry. This can be a really useful way of dealing with emotion. Take them to an area of privacy and allow them to cry for as long as they need to, offering only a tissue and firm support. Do not try to elicit details from them or try to engage in a conversation. No one cries for ever, and they will eventually cry themselves out. Crying is the body's natural reaction to shock, upset, anxiety and so forth, so don't berate them for it, but offer encouraging speech such as, 'Crying is cleansing and I think you needed to get that emotion out.'

If the emotion is anger then again try to steer them to an area away from other people in case they say something that they later regret, or try to draw others in. Do not mention the outburst, instead suggest that they take some deep breaths to help gain a sense of control and equilibrium. Acknowledge their anger, 'I understand you feel angry about all of this', but add a way forward, 'so I think a five-minute break might be helpful before we continue this conversation.' This statement has the added, but subtly understated, proviso that you will not be conversing until they calm down. As I have mentioned before, anger is a frightening emotion but it is not long lived. No one can stay in a state of anger for ever as it is immensely tiring, therefore your staff member will calm down, and you will then need to work with whatever behaviours remain (despair, sarcasm, a willingness to listen, and so forth).

Once you have dealt with the emotion, the resulting behaviour returns to behavioural management as detailed in Chapter 1. Poor behaviour can be managed through your organisational policies on behaviour. The main aspect is to ensure the communication continues. You will never resolve a situation if the communication stops.

Identifying core team objectives

One way of minimising the possibility of team discord is to set some core team objectives. Obviously this works well when everyone is working largely to a similar outcome, but it can also be helpful when people are doing very different tasks. It gives such people focus and a sense of being in a team when perhaps they had felt more like a specialist and a lone worker.

Whenever you set your team their objectives, whether this be at appraisal or any other time, the emphasis is often on creating individual objectives for each person. Objective setting does not have to be done this way. Several objectives can be set at team level and these are the objectives that everyone in the team shares responsibility for. This does not mean that everyone is doing the same thing. Although the objective is the same, the way in which each member fulfils it does not have to be. For example, you may decide that one of your core objectives for the team is:

To resolve every query put to the team within 48 hours.

For Mary this may be handling responses on the e-mail system, for John it is the phone enquiries and for Sarah it is the postal responses. While these are all from external sources Jim may handle the internal queries from other departments. All the team are achieving the same objective but by different methods and it is this striving for a common objective that bonds the team and gives them a common purpose.

Not all objectives need to be team ones. As part of appraisal you may have three objectives across the team and then each team member may have another three – or more – pertaining to themselves.

The last point about team objectives is that they should be written down in some way (to provide credibility) and may even be made into aspirational posters or form the basis of a customer charter for the team.

Reinforcing the benefits of a positive outcome

Teams are always on the flux. If they are working well as a team then any upset from one team member will affect everyone as there should be some group empathy taking place. That people should care for each other is natural. So there will always be ups and downs and imagining, therefore, that there is a team Nirvana out there is very unlikely to be realistic. However, you do need to have a big picture of how you would like the team to be. If you are to work together, for the good of the company, you need a vision. That vision is likely to see all your team enjoying the benefits of a healthy team support system. Anticipate that the team will have problems from time to time, but feel confident there is a range of solutions available to enable disputes to be reconciled and the team to be supported through their more difficult times.

Your view of the team may sound very obvious to you but unless you communicate it to the rest of the team, how will they know? You have been provided with a range of techniques throughout this book and your organisation will have policies in place to resolve situations between staff. However, none of them will be any good unless you are aware of them, use them and make the team aware of them also. Throughout all difficult situations and when dealing with difficult team members always stress your belief in a positive outcome. This will give everyone faith and hope that, whatever the problem, it can be resolved effectively, and the team can move forwards.

One final point to note is that, when you work through difficulties, it can make you much stronger. You will learn more about your team (and yourself) this way than by sailing through untroubled waters.

Conclusion

Both working in and managing teams can be very rewarding, however always anticipate that at some point some behaviour will need addressing – and ensure that you can handle it. This awareness of human nature together with a strong positive vision will set you in good store. It is only by being an exceptional communicator yourself that you can handle team dynamics. Very often the outward manifestation of the problem is not the actual cause at all and that, together with volatile and uncommunicative behaviour, makes it difficult to see inside many problems. However, you can only deal with the presenting behaviour until someone explains the detail, and then you need to be aware of the emotional fall out.

Emotions are a natural reaction to many situations so if that is an area where you feel you may come unstuck, find a training course that deals with this so that you feel confident with your own reaction. There are many training courses (or independent facilitators) that will help you (and the team) work through major issues. Help is never far away and as you grow in skills, you will grow in confidence.

Your Twelve-Point Tool Box

In this chapter I have proposed a number of solutions and aspects you need to consider.

To begin with you may like to think through some general techniques that can help you deal with many difficult situations, a Twelve-Point Tool Box of ideas and techniques that have been discussed and demonstrated throughout this book:

1 **Don't take it personally or get personal.** Anger or emotion will flow but it is rarely about you personally, it is about the situation. Never allow the altercation to become personal on either side as it makes discussions to find a solution almost impossible.

2 **Plan for emotion, it is only natural.** People seem terrified of emotion but it is only natural, up to a point. Never accept any form of violence. If you feel uneasy about how to handle the general emotions of others (crying, sadness, despondency and so forth), have a strategy in place for each. Expect emotions rather than see them as something of a surprise, then you are ready to deal with them more effectively.

3 **Listen, acknowledge, validate.** What the other person is saying is important. Exercise active listening. Acknowledge their concerns (although never accept blame at this stage). Validate their feelings. Use speech such as, 'If this is what has happened I can see how it would have made you upset. Let me look into this and then we can speak again.'

4 **Be calm and assertive.** If you all become excited by emotions you will not be thinking straight. Stay as calm as you can and model supportive body language. Don't be afraid to be assertive, you are the manager after all. If the conversation seems to be going around and around, or is no longer productive, someone needs to curtail it, and that someone is you. Don't ask, tell. Say something like, 'I have noted down the main points and I really need to look into this now. Let's meet to discuss this again later today/tomorrow.'

5 **Putting the onus on yourself.** Quite often many difficult people are bound up in themselves and their own feelings. To change focus or take the heat out of them, put the onus on yourself. Saying something such as, 'Let's check that I've been clear.' Suddenly, this makes the conversation about you, and that makes it more easy to control.

6 **Leave them the bus fare home.** Allow others either to withdraw their comments, apologise or change their minds with their dignity intact. It helps no one to crush people, show them up in front of others or expose them to ridicule. That will only cause long-term bad feeling from which you may never recover.

7 **Make a break – changing body language.** When things get very heated, the mind and the body work together and get locked. When people are angry you often see them rooted to the spot or, if they are upset, they may glue themselves into a chair. In essence, to maintain concentration on their feelings, people often get stuck in one physical position. Get them to change that position and it can change the way they think. Ask them to come with you to another room or move over to another chair. It can 'unstick' their thinking.

8 **Take ten.** If things become very heated or overly emotional, call for a break. Get a coffee, take a walk and return to the situation anew. It is amazing how different things seem after a ten-minute break.

9 **Own your feelings.** When speaking use first person language such as, 'I think' or 'This is how it affects me'. It is much more powerful than 'people think' or 'I've heard on the grapevine that you ...', which cannot be proven or justified.

10 **Levelling technique.** The power ratio in dealing with difficult situations can easily be unfairly balanced, with the manager holding most of the cards. Unless you want to rule by fear you need to level out this balance of power. Start by encouraging mutual feedback and open discussion and

if you have handled a situation particularly well, be open to accepting feedback on your own performance.

11 **Know the 'rules' in your company.** Every company has its own policies, rules and culture. Learn them and abide by them, otherwise you could find a difficult situation with someone else rebounding on you. A manager is judged not only on their own performance but also on how they interact and get the best out of others. Get it wrong and you could find yourself out of the door instead of the protagonist.

12 **Stay positive.** You have lived and worked with people all your life and that is great grounding for dealing with any difficult situation. You will not be able to solve everything for everyone but you need to be able to look in the mirror every night and know you handled things in the best way that you could.